GODLY RESPONSE TO HURT

Godly Response to Hurt

Being hurt may not be your fault, but your response is always your choice.

IFEOLUWA ADEFARAKAN

GLOEM, CANADA

CONTENTS

~ ~

Dedication

1

~ ~

Acknowledgement

3

~ ~

Introduction

5

~ chapter one ~

WHAT IS HURT?

7

~ chapter two ~

CAUSES OF HURT

9

~ chapter three ~

SYMPTOMS OF A HURTING LIFE

15

~ chapter four ~
UNGODLY RESPONSES TO HURT
19

~ chapter five ~
GODLY RESPONSES TO HURT
23

~ ~

YOU ARE NOT SAFE IF YOU ARE NOT SAVED
37

~ ~

About the Author
39

DEDICATION

I dedicate this book to God Almighty for His goodness towards me. And to my husband – my Best Friend – for encouraging me to share this with everyone.

Also to my son, David, for being a good boy in allowing me to have the time to write this book. You are the best boy alive.

Lastly, I dedicate this book to all my readers, and to everyone who is hurting at the moment, my heart goes out to you all.

ACKNOWLEDGEMENT

I sincerely acknowledge the Almighty God, Who alone is the Source of all wisdom. He is the Author and Finisher of my faith and it is of His fullness that the contents of this book have been drawn.

Also, I want to profoundly appreciate my dear parents – Late Chief and Mrs. Johnson Omojola – for the wonderful education foundation I was given. They taught me discipline, love, manners, respect and so much more; all of which have helped me succeed in life. Since my Dad passed into glory, Mom has been my great supporter. She's the strongest woman I know. Thank you so much for your relentless prayers. I cherish you Mom.

My most special appreciation goes to my darling husband, Oluwaseunmi; without his help this book might not have become a reality. I am so privileged to have him supervise the preparation and publishing of this book. My love, I appreciate your guidance, encouragement and the support you give at all times. Thank you so much. I love you!

To my siblings, I say a very big thank you for your love at all times. Knowing you are always there for me has been a great source of encouragement. I cherish our moments together: family love is everything.

And finally to my Uncles, Aunts and Friends; thank you all for your advice and prayers.

INTRODUCTION

In my few years on earth, I have experienced hurt in several dimensions. I have met with hurting people, seen what hurt can do to a person, and the most beautiful part is that I have also seen how God has used my hurting moments to bring out the best in me: what I call the blessedness of hurting moments. You will read about some of those moments as you read on.

Hurting moments are vulnerable moments; which explains why many people don't think things through before they react. Negative emotions such as anger, malice, bitterness, resentment, revenge etc are common reactions when one is hurting. But as God's children, we are not called to respond that way. There are better ways to respond to hurt according to God's design; and that's the essence of this book.

In this book, I will be sharing with you some causes of hurt, the symptoms of a hurting life, the wrong ways to handle hurting moments, and I will also be showing you how to choose godly response to hurt by considering some Bible Characters as well as others in our present day world who were hurt at one time or the other and the ways they responded.

I implore you to please read this book with an open heart because I am so sure the Lord wants to speak to you through it. And when you are through reading it, kindly say the prayer that follows with all sincerity. You will receive the touch of God.

Be blessed as you read on, and remember to tell those hurting around you about *Godly Response to Hurt.*

Ifeoluwa A. Adefarakan

~ Chapter One ~

WHAT IS HURT?

Hurt is a state of helplessness you feel when you have been or are being treated wrongly by someone; be it a family member, friends, colleagues, in-laws etc. A dictionary has described it (hurt, hurting) as feeling or suffering bodily or mental pain/distress. But in this book, our focus will be on the mental pain aspect.

In hurting moments, the heart is filled with sadness, tiredness, feelings of being cheated, incapacitation, and helplessness (especially for people with good hearts). On the other hand, those with hard hearts resolve to hatred, cursing, looking for ways to retaliate, etc.

Hurt may occur through misunderstanding or even through deliberate actions; and the last thing that comes to mind when one is hurting is forgiveness. As humans, we don't think about forgiveness at such moments. Rather, we look for ways to make our offenders feel what they have made us feel.

Take for instance the story of Samson in Judges 16: 28-30. He felt cheated and betrayed by what Delilah and her people did to him (even though it was partly as a result of his carelessness). The only thing that was on his mind was revenge; and being a natural response to hurt, his judgment was clouded at that moment. He couldn't think of anything else. So when he finally had an opportunity to pray, instead of asking God for strength to break loose from the chains his enemies had tied him with after gouging out his eyes, and to be restored in order to fulfill his purpose in life, he asked for strength to carry out revenge and also to die with his enemies. That's how people tend to pray when they are hurting. They offer blind prayers.

Personally, revenge has never felt good. It may taste sweet at the moment but given a little time, it will leave one with a certain inward unrest (especially if one is a child of God).

Romans 12:19 (GNT) says *"Never take revenge my friends, but instead let God's anger do it, for the scripture says 'I will take revenge, I will pay back, says the Lord'"*.

Later on in this book, we will learn how to respond to hurt in a godly way.

~ Chapter Two ~

CAUSES OF HURT

There are several factors capable of causing hurt; ranging from the seemingly little things to the big ones. The list of these causes is practically inexhaustive. But in this book we shall be considering some of the very common causes. It is very important to be able to identify what causes hurt in order to guard our hearts whenever they show up. The following are some of the identified causes;

Expecting too much from People
The popular saying - 'we are all humans' - is true and we can all relate with it. After all, blood runs in all humans and as such no man is beyond making mistakes.
With this knowledge, it is important to learn to make excuses for others when they offend us. Doing this ahead in our hearts will help us to overlook offences when they actually happen.
Consider the case of Jesus and Peter. Well before Peter denied Him after his arrest, Jesus had already prayed for him and forgiven him. That's why when Jesus looked at him upon his third denial, He didn't judge or condemn him. He only wanted him to realize that he could make mistakes even as a close associate. And immediately, Peter got the message. He was very sad but he repented and obtained mercy (Luke 22:31-34; Matthew 26:69-75).
We too can pray for people and forgive them well ahead of any per-

ceived offence.

Expecting too much from people as if they can never fail is an invitation to hurt.

Lack of Patience

Patience is the ability to accept or tolerate delay, trouble or suffering without getting angry or upset. It took me years before I accepted that I was not a patient person. Patience is truly a virtue. Most times after getting angry, in my moment of reflection I would realize I shouldn't have allowed things to go that far. I would realize that if I had been a little patient, I would have been able to prevent a fight or a heated argument.

Proverbs 16:32 (GNT) says *"It is better to be patient than powerful. It is better to win control over yourself than over cities"*.

Even if people see you as weak when you are operating in patience, just know in your heart that you are the strongest and the wise one. Patience is a sign of maturity; and as believers, we are supposed to keep growing in patience. If not, we will keep getting hurt.

Unmet Expectations

This happens when you are expecting something(s) from someone (either promised or pledged), and somehow, you get disappointed because they fail to fulfill their promises.

You can really be hurt by this because most times, such expectation must have built up your hope. Then you watch everything crashing down like a weak wall. It can be very frustrating. One lesson here though, our hope must always be in God, and not in human beings.

Betrayal

Betrayal according to a dictionary is the action of betraying one's country, a group or a person.

These days, betrayal is such a common phenomenon. Friends betraying friends, spouses betraying each other, Pastors betraying their congregations etc.

Usually we confide in people and share our secrets with them; and then when we hear those secrets from someone else we feel betrayed and as a result we become seriously hurt. At other times, the very people we share our secrets with get angry at us and expose our 'nakedness' to the whole world by broadcasting publicly what was meant to be kept as a secret.

Consider the story of Judas Iscariot's betrayal. He was one of the close followers of Jesus; but he took some money from those who wanted his master dead and revealed his location and identity to aid his arrest without giving it any second thought.

If you have friends who are showing signs of betrayal may be through gossips and backbiting, my sincere advice to you is this; do not reveal too much information about yourself when talking with them. Or better still, just stay away from them.

My husband usually says **we are commanded as Christians to love everyone, not to have friendship with everyone.**

Misinterpretation of Gestures

This is what I call jumping into conclusion about a person based on our perceptions; and it is very wrong. I used to do this a lot at some point in my life; especially when in emotionally vulnerable positions like staying with someone or having unresolved issues with my spouse.

For some reasons, once I am around someone and their face looks angry, devoid of love and joy, I quickly conclude that they are frowning at me or hardening their face to make me sad and I become hurt as a result.

But you see, most of the times I was proven wrong. By the time I summoned courage to ask what was going on with them, I got answers that were completely different from my perception. It's either they were battling with an unfinished project which they wished were completed in their mind or they were just dealing with some personal stuffs in their lives at the moment. So, I learnt to always ask whenever possible to know what's wrong when I see a sad or hard face instead of jumping into conclusions like I used to do. I have great peace doing this, and it saves me lots of headaches.

Death of a Loved One

Losing someone close to one's heart is a very painful experience to go through; and most times it is difficult to even explain the hurt.

I remember when I lost my Dad as a teenager, the pain was so much that I couldn't just process it. There were times I caught myself laughing or being happy months after his death; but then a sense of guilt would quickly wash over me suggesting that I didn't have the right to be happy, but to be mourning. This went on for a long time until I started learning to give my pains to God. That is, giving my burdens to Him and taking His yoke upon myself; and gradually I was healed.

But then some years later, I lost a very dear aunt of mine and it was as if my pains came all over again. I was deeply hurt within. I tried talking about my pains to close friends, though that helped a little, yet the hurt was still there. I had to lean on God fully before I could get over it.

False Accusations

This brings to mind the story of Joseph in the Bible when his master's wife falsely accused him of rape according to Genesis 39. It was an unpalatable experience for Joseph because not only was he denied the opportunity to defend himself, he was also imprisoned for a crime he never committed. He must have been deeply hurt, but God was with him all through so he was able to pull through.

I also have had my share of false accusations; and at one of such times, I just couldn't find the right words to defend myself, so all I did was cry. Every attempt I made to explain myself was countered with more negative words, and I tell you the truth, it was so hurtful. Some people have been falsely accused by their so called friends and all of a sudden they find themselves estranged to their once upon a time good friends. They consider the way they are now being treated and can't help but wonder what has happened to the trust they once shared.

And then, there are some currently serving jail terms (like the case of Joseph mentioned earlier) as a result of false accusations while their accusers are walking about freely. Later on in this book we will see how to handle such.

Financial Loss (Failed Investments)

Entrepreneurs or people who are into business and investments will understand this better. Recording a great loss of money as a result of a failed investment is very hurtful. It is not uncommon for investors caught in such unfortunate situations to sometimes contemplate suicide. Thoughts of other ways they could have invested to avoid the mess at hand would suddenly fill their minds; but then it would have been too late because money is lost already. However, with God's help as we will soon see, beauty can still come out of those ashes.

Maltreatment

The feeling that comes with being maltreated especially by one's close friend or spouse can be very hurtful. At such moments, one can't seem to find any logical explanation to what's really happening. And it's especially painful because the maltreatment is coming from someone who is supposed to be your partner and confidant.

At other times, it may be your boss at work who suddenly decides to make your life miserable for no justifiable reason, and you begin to wonder why it has to be you. Also, in a home where love, care and affection are absent, the children might end up being maltreated. And being a hurtful experience, the children might grow up with low self-esteem and hearts full of hatred.

Ill Health

When someone who has been healthy suddenly falls ill and it becomes so severe, such a person might start asking the popular question: Why did God allow this to happen to me? Or why does it have to be me? Not getting answers to these questions and having to deal with such health conditions can be very hurtful. Just imagine a cancer patient. There's nothing beautiful about such an illness.

These are just to mention a few as there are many other causes of hurt. In the next section, we will be considering the symptoms of a hurting life.

~ Chapter Three ~

SYMPTOMS OF A HURTING LIFE

The following have been identified as symptoms characterizing a hurting life;

Absence of Love
Bitterness eats deep into the life of a hurting person, graduating into an ideology of being withdrawn sort of. And because of this, they find it very hard to show love to themselves let alone to those around them. There is no way love can be perfect when there are weights attached to it and dragging it down. 1 John 4:18 says *"There is no fear in love; perfect love drives out all fear..."*

When hurting, it will be very difficult to love people even in the simplest way. This is usually because you will find it uneasy to love yourself at such moments, and you can't give what you don't have. The Bible says love your neighbors as yourself; so God expects us to love ourselves genuinely and then transfer same to our neighbors. Your self-love is very important; and unfortunately it's one of the very first things that hurt attacks.

For me, I tell myself I am the best version of me because God created me uniquely. No one has the exact type of my genetic make-up in the whole universe; and this always encourages me to be the best at what I do. The same is true for you too. You are one of a kind.

Fear

A hurting person seems to exhibit fear most of the time. Even after enjoying a moment of relief, the fear of being let down again keeps them in anxiety as they begin to suspect everyone around them. This degenerates further until they literally find it difficult to trust anyone again. What a pathetic way to live!

Lack of Confidence

When a person is hurting, their self-confidence seems to get eroded. They suddenly lose the courage to try something new because they are afraid of failing or worse still, the bitterness in their hearts as a result of people's attitude towards them may force them to remain in their shell. It is a feeling of insecurity, anxiety and uncertainty.

Self- Pity

This is what happens when all you do is focus on negative feelings brought about by the bad things that are happening or that are being done to you. It is a state of feeling sorry for oneself or being overly sad about hurtful situations. You look to others to care for you and show you some compassion because you've got no self-worth left.

Unforgiveness

This is a very common symptom of a hurting life. When you are hurt, forgiveness isn't usually part of your options. All you can think about at that moment is to make the one who hurt you feel the same pain you are feeling. To be happy about other people's happiness becomes so difficult and unless God intervenes, it may degenerate into something more terrible.

Other symptoms include prolonged sadness, lack of compassion etc. And if care is not taken, all these symptoms can birth certain dangerous situations such as making wrong decisions, depression, murder or even suicide.

~ Chapter Four ~

UNGODLY RESPONSES TO HURT

These refer to the natural ways we tend to respond to hurt which are not in any way pleasing to God. They are what many will refer to as expected responses when one is hurting. These ungodly responses include;

1. **Revenge:** the action of inflicting hurt or harm on someone for an injury or wrong suffered at their hands.
2. **Bitterness:** anger and disappointment at being treated unfairly; resentment.
3. **Jealousy:** which generally refers to the thoughts or feelings of insecurity, fear, and concern over a relative lack of possessions or safety. It can consist of one or more emotions such as anger, resentment, inadequacy, helplessness or disgust.
4. **Constantly harboring evil thoughts towards the offender:** thinking and wishing something bad will happen to the offender.
5. **Malice:** the intention or desire to do evil; ill will towards the offender; often manifesting as conscious avoidance of any form of communication with the offender.
6. **Character assassination:** the malicious and unjustified harming of a person's good reputation. Destroying the of-

fender's public image as a way of getting back for the wrong done.

These and the likes are all ungodly responses to hurt; but let's talk a little more about bitterness and jealousy.

Bitterness
Bitterness is associated with hurt; and as a matter of fact, hurt is what fertilizes bitterness, making it grow almost uncontrollably like weed. Its root goes down into the heart, and when anger together with resentment keeps watering it, it spreads more and more until it hardens one's spirit.

Hebrews 12:14-15 (GNT) says *"Try to be at peace with everyone and try to live a holy life, because no one will see the Lord without it. Guard against turning back from the grace of God, let no one become like a bitter plant that grows up and causes many troubles with its poison."*

As earlier defined, bitterness is anger and disappointment at being treated unfairly; resentment. Going by this definition, it is advisable to deal with bitterness at the early stage because if not well managed, it may result in death at the end of the day.

Jealousy
Jealousy is also one of the products of bitterness; and people have killed because of it. The Bible says in Proverbs 14:30 that *"Peace of mind makes the body healthy but jealousy is like a cancer"*. And what does cancer do? It eats up everything in its way and eventually damages the whole body, usually resulting in death.

Take for instance the story of Cain and Abel in Genesis 4: 1-16 (GNT). The Bible was careful to mention that Cain became furious and he growled in anger (bitterness). Something was happening which Cain was not happy about; so what did he do?

You see, our reactions to occurrences or situations in our lives matter a lot. Things might happen to us, making us unhappy; but it is how we react to them that matters the most.

Verses 6 and 7 made us realize the effort God made to help Cain; He didn't judge him right away. He asked him *"Why are you angry? Why that scowl on your face? If you had done the right thing, you would be smiling; but because you have done evil, sin is crouching at your door. It wants to rule you, but you must overcome it."*

With this effort, God was trying to call his attention to what He had seen in his heart which he was about to carry out - killing his brother; but he wouldn't listen and he eventually killed Abel. Cain graduated from anger to bitterness, from bitterness to jealousy and from jealousy to murder.

In this life, we will feel hurt at one point or the other, either through the actions of those close to us or outsiders. Whichever way it comes, our response in such moments is what matters, and it's also what determines how everything will eventually turn out. Always remember this: **'No one can hurt you without your permission.'**

~ Chapter Five ~

GODLY RESPONSES TO HURT

In this chapter, the Lord will be opening our eyes to the right responses to hurt. By godly, it means these responses are pleasing to God; and practically applying them in our lives will bring Him nothing but joy.

Before we consider these responses, it is very important to note that there is one major factor that can make these happen; it is called GRACE. Nobody can respond correctly to hurt unless grace is at work. And grace has been defined as an unmerited favor, goodwill and loving-kindness especially as granted by a superior to an inferior, like God towards us (His children). Grace isn't something you work for; you are just given in good faith, without expecting any pay back.

Most times we are hurt because our focus is on the offender or the offence. We need to learn how to focus on God at such moments. He is the only One Who knew about the situation long before it happened (Isaiah 46:10). Also, He is definitely the only One Who knows why it happened in the first place and no other person knows the way out of it except Him. That's why whenever we are hurt, irrespective of who the offender is – your sister, brother, parent, friends, spouse, colleagues etc, the first Person to talk to about it is God. Pour out your heart to Him. Tell Him exactly the way you feel; and it's very much okay to even cry when telling Him. You will sense His grace being released upon you to enable you overcome or deal with the hurt. That's the approach that pleases Him so well. It shows your absolute dependence on Him.

Let's consider how some Bible Characters dealt with their hurts. Their godly responses are worthy of emulation.

Joseph [Genesis 37 – 42]

The first Bible Character we want to consider is Joseph as recorded in Genesis 37 – 42.

Joseph was much loved by his father because he was the son of his old age, and he made him a coat of many colors. However, when his half-brothers noticed the special attention and affection he enjoyed from their father, they became consumed with jealousy and hatred. To make matters worse, God gave Joseph a dream about his future greatness which he shared with his brothers out of excitement; and that increased their levels of hatred for him because they felt insulted and bitter that he was going to be greater than them. Now, it is to be noted that Joseph was uniquely known for his dreams because that was how he felt God communicated with him.

One day, his father sent him to go check on his brothers who were out working in the field; so he went. But upon seeing him afar off, his jealous brothers felt they had had enough of him and wanted to kill him until one of them suggested something different. They eventually agreed to sell him into slavery and make a good fortune from the transaction; and that's what they did. Joseph was only 17 years old when his own blood brother did this to him. Imagine his pain and unhappiness. Now let's face it, he had every reason in the world to be angry at his brothers for life, considering their wickedness towards him. They forcefully took away his teen/early adulthood years from him as he ended up in Egypt as a serving slave.

At this point as humans, the only thing that should be going on in his head was how he was going to get back at his brothers; exposing them for who they were and dealing with them in any way possible. But the Bible didn't say so; rather it was careful to mention that even in slavery 'the Lord was with Joseph'. It was all part of His big and beautiful plans for him (Jeremiah 29:11). Joseph's ordeal continued for 13 years before the Lord supernaturally intervened and made him the first Prime Minister of Egypt (from being a slave to being in charge of a whole nation) –Genesis 41:40-46.

After some time, there was a global famine and Egypt was the only place where people could get food. So Jacob (Joseph's father) sent his sons (Joseph's brothers) to go buy some food in Egypt. But when they arrived and discovered it was Joseph who was in charge of the nation and the food distribution, they became so afraid because they felt Joseph (now in a powerful position) was going to punish them for what they did to him years ago. The only thing on their mind was how Joseph was going to use his imperial power to order their execution. But Joseph gave them the greatest shock of their lives; instead of seeking revenge, he spoke kindly to them according to Genesis 45:5, 8 (CJB) – *"But now do not be sad, and let it not trouble you that you sold me here, for it was to preserve life that God sent me before you...you did not send me here, but God..."*

Joseph recognized that all the travails he had undergone were ordained by God to ensure the survival of Egypt and the surrounding nations (including his father's). Keeping that in mind enabled him to forgive his brothers and repay animosity with benevolence. As we said earlier, it was grace that helped Joseph to respond to his hurt in a godly manner. He knew God was with him all through so he chose to focus on Him rather than dwelling on his hurt. You too can decide to give all your hurts to God today and let Him work on you to bring out glory from your ashes.

Stephen [Acts 6 – 7]

The second Bible Character we want to consider is Stephen, as recorded in Acts 6 and 7. He was one of the first deacons to be appointed by the Twelve Apostles of Jesus Christ. He was a man full of faith and the Holy Spirit; and God used him to perform great miracles and wonders among the people. But the Bible made us realize in Acts 6:9 that he was opposed by some men (Jews) who were members of the synagogue together with some other Jews from different provinces. They started an argument with Stephen, but through the wisdom of God made available to him, he was able to answer them all. When they saw they couldn't refute him, they bribed some men to tell lies against him capable of getting him into trouble with the religious leaders.

How many of us can relate with that? Someone tells a lie against us or a group of people simply cooks up false stories about us and we find it so difficult to explain ourselves. At that very moment, trusting the Holy Spirit for the right words is the only wise option as He is the Spirit of wisdom and our only Defense. He might instruct us to be quiet for some minutes before saying anything or He may simply supply us with certain statements that will clear all the lies. The most important thing in all of these is to obey Him and not allow our flesh to dictate otherwise.

Still on the story of Stephen; by the time you get to Chapter 7 of Acts, he had been falsely accused and in spite of his explanations he was condemned to death by stoning. But while he was being stoned, the unusual happened. Instead of being bitter and raining curses on his accusers (which would have been the natural response to such an unfair treatment), Stephen knelt down and cried out in a loud voice (loud enough for his accusers to hear him) *"Lord! Do not remember this sin against them!" He said this and he died."* (Acts 7: 60). What a response! This could only have been by the grace of God. Despite the pain he was suffering as they were stoning him, all he could think of was to ask the Lord for their forgiveness. That was grace in its purest form.

Like Stephen who kept looking towards heaven when he was about to be killed (Acts 7:55-56), we too can pray for grace in our hurting moments to focus on Jesus rather than those hurting us. Now this is not going to be easy; but with God's help, it is possible. That's why it is called grace.

Asking God questions like *"What do You want to bring out of my situation?"* or *"How do You want me to respond in a way that will glorify You?"* are great approaches towards practicing godly response to hurt.

David [1 Samuel 18]

Another Character we will be looking at is David. The story about what transpired between young David and King Saul is a unique one.

In 1 Samuel 18, it was recorded that by reason of David's unprecedented victory over Goliath, he began to attract more accolades and praises from the people than the King himself. King Saul noticed this and became angry and jealous; he felt threatened by David's increasing popularity and he began looking for ways to kill him.

Several attempts were made on David's life, but because God was with him, he was able to escape all. As God's children, whenever anyone is trying to hurt us, we too should be assured of the Presence of God in our lives; and we should settle it in our minds that no matter what, God will always provide us with a way of escape. That's the essence of His faithfulness.

There was a time when David had the opportunity to kill King Saul. In the process of hunting David and his men down, the King became tired and decided to rest. David caught him sleeping and vulnerable; and his men urged him to kill the King once and for all so his life could get back to normal again. They even quoted some of the promises of God to David which fitted so well for the occasion. But David chose to repay evil with kindness and spared the life of King Saul – his sworn enemy. And because of that kindness he showed to his enemy, he had to keep running for his life because Saul didn't stop chasing him (even after realizing David spared his life).

Then something unusual happened; King Saul had died in battle (1 Samuel 31:1-13) and the report of his death got to David. Wasn't David supposed to roll out the drums and begin to rejoice that finally the man who had made life miserable for him had died? Not at all! As a matter of fact, according to 2 Samuel 1:11-12, David tore his clothes in sorrow when he had the news and grieved so much (together with all his men who had been running with him). As if that was not enough, he sang a song of lamentation for the King and his son (Jonathan) in 2 Samuel 1:17-27. He felt really sad and wept bitterly that his sworn enemy died. That means, when King Saul was busy chasing him up and down, looking for ways to kill him, David still had compassion for him. That was rather uncommon.

As God's children, we too can have the same attitude towards our persecutors; and we can be sure God will always vindicate us like He did for David.

Matthew 5:44 (KJV) says:

"But I say to you, love your enemies, bless them that curse you, do good to them that hate you and pray for them which despitefully use you, and persecute you."

Ruth [Ruth 1]

The next Character we will briefly be considering is Ruth, as recorded in Ruth 1.

Ruth was hurt by the loss of a loved one (one of the factors that lead to hurt); she lost her husband. But instead of brooding over her loss and wallowing in self-pity, she decided to look beyond her own pain and become the shoulder her mother-in-law (who was also in pain because of the death of her husband and two sons) could lean on. She could have stayed back in her town and explore her chances of remarrying, but she chose to return with Naomi (her mother-in-law) to her own town. She responded to her own hurt by helping that old woman overcome hers, even when it meant a very bleak future for her.

In her hurting moments, Ruth chose to operate in love; and as a result, the Lord rewarded her by giving her a good, godly and very wealthy husband (Ruth 4). She got married and became happy once again. She became a celebrity among her husband's people because of her good heart, and her dreams were fulfilled. Her decision to respond with love in her hurting moments paid off as she was rewarded with a fulfilled life. Our Lord and Savior Jesus Christ even came from her lineage (Matthew 1:1-17). What an honor!

Hannah [1 Samuel 1]

Lastly, we will be considering the life of Hannah as recorded in 1 Samuel 1. She suffered a great deal of mockery and maltreatment at the hands of her husband's other wife (Peninnah) because of her barrenness which was not in any way a fault of hers (it was God Who shut her womb – 1 Samuel 1:5); but she used a different approach to deal with her hurt. The Bible says Hannah would cry and refuse to eat anytime Peninnah mocked her; but she didn't stop there, she also continued to pray for divine intervention concerning her barrenness. That way, her focus was not on the hurt but on the God Who could end her reproach. And eventually, God remembered her and gave her a son (Samuel) who later grew to become a great Prophet and Israel's first kingmaker. To further compensate her for her ordeal and godly response to hurt, God gave her five more children; and the one who was mocked for being barren ended up becoming a mother of six. That's what God does when we honor Him by responding positively in our hurting moments.

In case you are the type who likes to cry whenever you are hurt instead of talking to God about it, you need to take a cue from Hannah. Being a highly emotional person with a soft heart and willingness to follow peace with all men, I cry when I'm hurt; but I don't just cry, I also talk to God about my reason(s) for crying. Like Hannah did, I pour out my heart to God, and from experience, I have seen Him helping me overcome the hurt at such moments. Now, several actions might follow this. I may be led to go meet the person hurting me and express myself in the best possible way, peradventure they don't really know how hurt I am; or if they are unapproachable, I just keep praying in my heart for God to heal me and to also touch their heart. And eventually, like God answered Hannah, I get my answers as well.

But then, there are some groups of people who feel hurt because they feel cheated by nature; their suffering has nothing to do with what anyone did to them. Are you in that category? Peradventure you feel cheated because you are naturally handicapped, or because you were born with some debilitating diseases and you are wondering why it has to be you. You are hurting because everyone else around you is fine and there you are, suffering from conditions you didn't do anything to deserve. Maybe this has even sapped all your happiness as you are constantly living with the hurt; I want to tell you that you can still respond positively. Yes, you can.

You see, God (your Maker) has a purpose and answer for everything that happens to you in this life. I remember the beautiful story of a woman who was once invited to my church. She was an active athlete as a teenager; but at age 17, she broke her neck in a diving accident, her spinal cord was severed and she became paralyzed from her shoulders down. After the accident, she became so angry, hurt and depressed that she even begged friends to help her commit suicide. Ultimately, she said she found peace when she committed her life to God; and for over 40 years now, she has been traveling around the world sharing her story and helping others overcome their hurts. Hallelujah! That's what God can do. He can bring out the best out of the worst situations if only we will allow Him.

Please, kindly look beyond your hurts and focus your attention mainly on God. He is a good God and all He does is good (Psalm 145:9).

All the Bible Characters we considered in this chapter were humans like us. But one thing stood out in their stories, the GRACE to respond rightly to their hurts was made available to them. And that's what I call the God-factor.

The God Who helped them is still very much willing to help anyone who dares to ask Him (Matthew 7:7). Please desire and pray for such grace today and I assure you, your life will not remain the same.

As we conclude this chapter, pay attention to these two additional qualities capable of helping you respond to hurt the way God wants you to. They are:

Patience
This is the ability to endure difficult situations without responding negatively. It is a very important virtue that we should all ask God for. It is not in any way a sign of weakness as some people think; rather, it is a sign of maturity. We need to grow in patience as believers so that whenever we face trials or troubles we can be able to respond rightly.
Patience is not a gift, it is a fruit (virtue) that requires daily cultivation if it must grow to a level where we are able to handle anything that comes our way calmly.

Proverbs 16:32 (GNT) says *"It is better to be patient than powerful. It is better to win control over yourself than over whole cities."* And Proverbs 19:11 (GNT) further says *"If you are sensible, you will control your temper. When someone wrongs you, it is a great virtue to ignore it."*

The true test of patience is how we respond when our rights are violated. Let us always remember this virtue called patience whenever we are hurt; we can never outgrow it. That's one way to ensure we respond well each time we are hurt. And you know one other good thing about patience? It helps one to see the bigger picture. Because it makes room for the passage of time, the heat gets to cool off and what was initially considered as hurt may actually not be hurtful as such. Time usually reveals things as they truly are.

And peradventure you are reading this book now and you know in your heart that you usually hurt people through your words, actions, attitudes etc., or you've had people approach you at one time or the other telling you that you hurt them, I want to implore you to kindly pay attention. It's different if you didn't know; but now you are aware. Make conscious efforts to avoid hurting people henceforth. You too need to learn to be patient in your interactions with others. Be sensitive to the emotions of the people around you.

If you are the type who loves to talk before thinking like I once was, try to be more patient in your responses to people or situations. There is a reason God gave us two ears and only one mouth. James 1:19 (GNT) says *"Remember this, my dear friends! Everyone must be quick to listen, but slow to speak and slow to become angry."* Let's not form the habit of apologizing again and again without changing our ways. Saying 'sorry' is good; but avoiding heated arguments and hurtful remarks in the first place is better.

It is also important for you to know that part of the healing process for some people might mean coming to you in person to talk about the hurt you caused them. If that happens, please be kind and patient enough to listen to them because most times it takes a lot of effort to do such. At the end, all that matters is to forgive, move on and forget the pain.

Forgiveness

Forgiveness in Greek simply means 'to let go'. It is the act of pardoning an offender. The Lord's Prayer in Luke 11: 4 says *'Forgive us our sins as we forgive those who sin against us'.*

We forgive others when we let go of resentment and give up any claim to be compensated for the hurt or loss we have suffered. The Bible teaches that unselfish love is the basis for true forgiveness, since love doesn't keep record of injury - 1 Corinthians 13:4-5.

How do we forgive someone who hurts us?

- **By remembering what forgiveness involves:** You are not condoning the wrong or acting as if it never occurred, you are simply letting go.
- **By recognizing the benefits of forgiveness:** Letting go of anger and resentment can help you keep calm, improve your health and as a result increase your level of happiness (Proverbs 14:30; Matthew 5:9). According to Matthew 6:14-15, forgiving others is what qualifies you to receive God's forgiveness for your own sins.
- **By being empathetic:** We are all imperfect, but working towards perfection (James 3:2). Just as you love being forgiven when you make mistakes, you should also forgive the mistakes of other people (Matthew 7:12).
- **And lastly, by acting quickly:** Please and please, work hard to forgive as soon as you can rather that allowing your anger to fester (Ephesians 4:26-27). Delaying to offer forgiveness is inviting God's judgment for your own sins.

There was this story of a man who lost his wife during childbirth. He was so sad, but then he took solace in seeing her daughter grow as years went by. That girl was everything to him and he wouldn't allow anything or anyone to hurt her.

After some time, the girl became mature enough to get married and she brought her suitor home to meet her dad. This man welcomed her daughter's suitor and begged him to take care of his daughter. He explained to him how much he cared about her and how much her happiness meant to him. The suitor agreed to take care of the girl and the man gave them his blessings.

They got married, and they started living together. But not long after their wedding, this young man began to maltreat his wife. He would shout at her, beat her up and even threaten to kill her. This girl had to run back to her father's house because she felt her husband was going to kill her.

When her father saw her, he became angry and so bitter at the young man, considering the fact that he begged him to treat his daughter well. In his anger, he vowed never to forgive his son-in-law.

Then after a while, the unusual happened. The man suddenly developed a sickness which led to the swelling of his entire body. He just kept swelling up. He tried to get medical help but every effort proved abortive as his tests didn't reflect anything useful. Finally, he decided to seek spiritual help, so he went for prayers. That was when the Lord revealed to him that his sickness was as a result of unforgiveness. He was told that someone offended him and he had vowed never to forgive the person. He was further told that the only way out of his mysterious sickness was to forgive the person. Right there, he knew it had to do with his son-in-law. So, he decided to visit him and communicate his forgiveness to him.

Upon opening the door and seeing his father-in-law, the young man was about to run away thinking he had come to kill him. But the man told him he had come to communicate his forgiveness. They both fell on each other's shoulders and wept. At that instant, the swelling disappeared. He got back to his normal size instantaneously. That's what forgiveness does. You are actually the one benefitting the most when you forgive.

Having said all these, please don't allow people to keep taking advantage of you. For example, someone borrows money from you, squanders it, and then comes back to you apologizing for being unable to pay back. Yes, you should forgive them by not harboring resentment or bitterness. However, wisdom demands that when such people come to you for loans at another time, you might want to consider loaning out an amount that won't hurt you or affect you in case they don't pay back. Or better still, you might want to give them what you can afford without expecting them to pay back (for your own peace of mind). You can give them what you can easily let go of and not feel bad about it (Proverbs 14:15; 22:3; Galatians 6:7).

My humble prayer is that the grace to do all these without any form of struggle be released upon us abundantly in the Name of Jesus. Amen.

So are you hurting today? Say this prayer with me:

"Dear Heavenly Father, I thank You for saving my life. Thank You for loving me unconditionally and thank You for teaching me from your Word. I open up my heart to You today Lord, please fill me with Your love and peace. I lay down every hurt in my life at the cross of Calvary and I pray that You take up my burdens and heal my heart. Help me to live my life patterned after Your love and help me to be able to love unconditionally like You without holding back. This I pray and I believe I receive in Jesus' Name. Amen."

Congratulations; your healing shall be permanent in Jesus' Name. Welcome to a New Beginning!

If you need further help or you just want to reach out, please feel free to do so via this email address: ifeoluwaomojola@yahoo.com

YOU ARE NOT SAFE IF YOU ARE NOT SAVED

ACCEPT THE SALVATION JESUS CHRIST OFFERS TODAY!

Did you notice that throughout this book I placed so much emphasis on responding to hurt in a way that pleases God? It's because He is the only One Who can really help the hurting. Counselors, Psychologists, Social Workers and even Pastors may try their best in helping you recover from your hurts, but the ultimate healing and restoration you need can only come from the One Who created your heart. He is your Manufacturer, and no one understands a product better than the Manufacturer.

So if you have not yet surrendered your life to Jesus Christ, you are missing a lot; and it is so dangerous because the devil won't stop afflicting you with all manners of hurts until he finally claims your life.

There is no way you are going to enjoy the joy and peace Jesus offers to His own unless you become connected to Him.

If you will like to surrender your life to Jesus Christ, say this prayer now:

"Lord Jesus, I am a sinner and I cannot help myself. Please wash me in your precious blood and make me a new creature. I open the door of my heart to you today, come into my life and become my Lord and Savior. Grant me the grace to overcome the devil and my hurts;

prepare me for eternity and help me to escape the judgment reserved for sinners. Thank You Jesus for saving me. Amen."

ABOUT THE AUTHOR

Ifeoluwa is a Canadian author experienced in helping people overcome their hurts by the grace of God. Born and raised in Nigeria, she has always been passionate about helping people through counselling, mentorship, prayers and giving.

She served in the Evangelism department and later became the Welfare Coordinator of her Campus fellowship - Redeemed Christian Fellowship - during her university years. This was another opportunity for her to channel her energy towards helping others.

However, in 2011 she became fully aware that God had called her into the Helps Ministry and that realization has been fueling her passion ever since.

Godly Response to Hurt is one of the ways she has decided to help more people overcome their pains and emotional breakdowns. Through this book, she shares some of the ways God has been able to help her lead a more peaceful, contented and happy life over the years. She is the wife of the President of Global Emancipation Ministries – Calgary [GLOEM], Canada.

She is blissfully married, and her marriage is fruitful to the glory of God.

www.ingramcontent.com/pod-product-compliance
Lightning Source LLC
Chambersburg PA
CBHW041217070526
44583CB00001B/13